Reach Around Books Season Two...

Who Will Help Jack Off the Horse?
Brenda's Beaver Plays a Round
JiggleWiggleTicklePickle
Lucy Lickalotopus Goes Down South
Peter Pitched a Tent

Reach Around Books Season One...

Suzy Likes to Look at Balls
Come Swing with Us!
Put Tony's Nuts in Your Mouth!
Spank the Monkey Lends a Hand
Brenda's Beaver Needs a Barber

www.ReachAroundBooks.com

Season 2 Book 5

Peter Pitched a Tent

written by Bimisi Tayanita

illustrated by Sumguyen Bangladesh

created by Matt Williams, Inmate #030820269

This is a work of fiction. Names, characters and incidents are products of the author's imagination and are used fictitiously. Any resemblance to actual events or persons (living or dead) is entirely coincidental...Except for Peter, I told him I'd write a book about him if he covered one of my early morning shifts throwing bags at the airport.

Copyright ©2020 Reach Around Books, LLC.
PO BOX 910555 Saint George UT 84791

All rights reserved. This book or any portion thereof may not be reproduced or used in any manner whatsoever without the express written permission of the publisher.

ISBN 978-1-946178-11-4   First printing   Printed with love, in China.

"Peter Pitched a Tent" is the fifth of five books that make up Season Two.

www.ReachAroundBooks.com

Peter dreams of camping,
             with mermaids by the sea

Sometimes one, sometimes two...
last night he dreamed of three

When grandma came to wake him up
back out the door she went

At some point in the night it seems that Peter pitched a tent

Peter is excitable,
    he loves the great outdoors

He built a campsite in the night,
    right on his bedroom floor

He's no good at chopping wood. He's terrible at fishing. The skills that make a camper good... Peter's mostly missing.

He has more pimples on his face than he has camping sense. But, Peter is a total ace when it comes to pitching tents.

He took down the tent that he had pitched and headed off to school

Along the way he had an itch to stop off at the pool

Peter timed it perfectly,
    such a stroke of luck

The senior female diving team was practicing their tucks

Peter pitched a tent with ease...
much larger than before

This show of swimming expertise could not be ignored

Peter's friends, Matt and Zack were waiting at the school

Both of them sat back and laughed
when he told 'em 'bout the pool

Peter likes the science teacher,
in her class he's never bored

She was showing off some creature when it hopped down to the floor

She turned her back to pick it up and bent down on one knee...

In three seconds flat, his tent was up;
a towering tee-pee!

After school, Matt and Peter
   came to hang with Zack

Zack's front yard was getting lame,
so they headed towards the back

Right there in their swimwear,
 in front of everyone

Zack's mom and his sister were laying in the sun

Zack announced "It's time to go!"
But when he turned around

Matt sat down to watch the show
...as the circus came to town

Peter started twitching. He was turning red.
The circuits all were glitching deep inside his head.
He sputtered and he wheezed...
　　　　his eyes were rolling back

When finally he breathed, everyone stepped back

Zack's sister still is not convinced that he is just thirteen...

Peter pitched the biggest tent the world has ever seen!

Spank the Monkey's on his way to visit Petertown
He's gonna need a helping hand
...to take that big tent down!

Egogahan.

...because "the end" is too final.